SAVE THE LIBRARY!

by Katie Dale and Nigel Baines

W

FRANKLIN WATTS

LONDON·SYDNEY

CHAPTER 1

Summer loved the library. Every Wednesday she took back the books she'd read, and borrowed new ones. The librarian, Jan, smiled as Summer walked in with her mum. "I loved the book. Thank you for helping me choose it, Jan," said Summer. "It was brilliant."

"You're welcome," said Jan.

"But I won't be able to help for much longer.

The library is closing down."

"OH NO!" Summer gasped. "It can't!" she cried.

"Even if I saved up all my pocket money, I would

never be able to buy all the books I want

to read!"

WE ARE
CLOSING SOON

"I have to save the library! But what can I do?"
Summer asked, sitting at a computer.

"Why don't you hold a protest?" said Mum.

"What's that?" Summer asked.

"It's when a lot of people get together to show
they want to change something," said Mum.

"You could make a poster, telling people where and when to meet up," said Mum.

"Good idea!" said Summer. She quickly designed a poster. Then she printed lots of copies and stuck them up all over town.

CHAPTER 2

But that night it rained hard. The next morning,

most of the posters were soggy and unreadable.

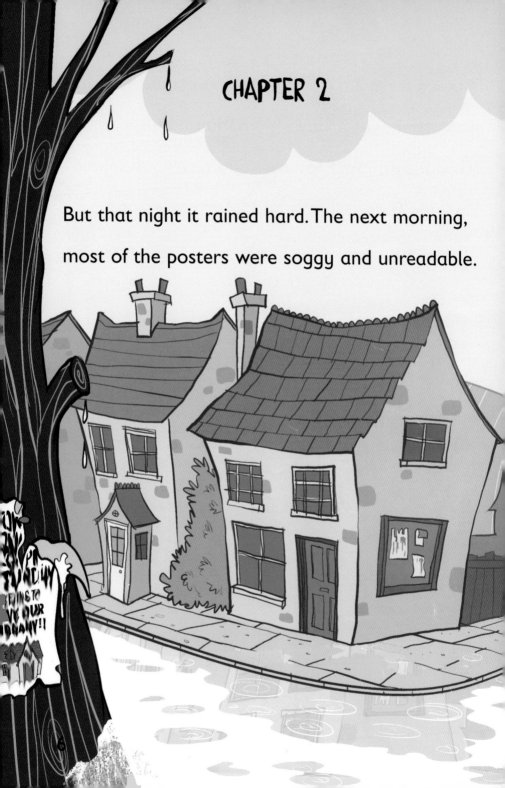

"Never mind, we'll put up new ones when you come home," said Mum.

"My friends will help," said Summer, and she hurried into school.

"The library is going to close. We need to save it! It's the only local library we have," Summer told her friends, I-Lin, Karen and Arvind. But her friends didn't seem bothered.

"I don't use the library," said I-Lin. "I always read on my phone. Books are too heavy."

"I prefer watching DVDs," added Karen.

"But we need the library to look up facts!" said Summer.

"I use the internet to do that," Arvind replied.

"But ..." Summer didn't know what to say. Didn't any of her friends need the library like she did?

After school, Summer and her mum
put up more posters with plastic sleeves
to keep them dry.

TOWN
SQUARE
3·00PM
SATURDAY
MEETING TO
SAVE OUR
LIBRARY!!

"What if no one turns up?" said Summer when

they got home.

"Cheer up, Summer," said Mum. "I bought

your favourite cake for tea.

Everyone likes cake!"

That gave Summer an idea ...

CHAPTER 3

"It's not just a protest anymore," Summer told her friends the next day. "There's going to be a cake sale too! Will you come now?"

"Sorry Summer," I-Lin said. "I have band practice."

"And I'm visiting my cousin," added Karen.

"I can't come either," Arvind sighed. "Mum says
I have to redo the space poster I did
for homework because I got the facts wrong."

After school, Summer baked cupcakes, flapjacks and brownies. They looked wonderful and smelled even better. Bongo agreed!

"Get down, Bongo," Summer said, pulling him away. "These cakes are for the cake sale!"

But the next morning Summer found Bongo eating all her cakes!

"Bongo, stop!" Summer cried, but it was too late. "Now there are no cakes for me to sell, and it's raining. No one will come to the protest!"

"Come on, Summer," Mum said, comforting her. "We have to try."

Summer nodded. Even if no one else turned up, she'd do her best to save the library.

CHAPTER 4

When Summer reached the town square, her jaw dropped. It was filled with hundreds of people.

"Save our library!" they all chanted loudly.

"Hi Summer," Arvind called.

"There isn't any cake." Summer sighed.

"I'm not here for cake," Arvind laughed. "I'm here to save our library!"

"Mum said I got my space facts wrong because I didn't check them in a book," Arvind explained. "She said if I'd gone to the library that wouldn't have happened, so we've come to help save it!"

"Hi Summer," Karen called, running over with a little girl. Summer gasped. "I thought you were visiting your cousin?"

"I was. But when I told her about your protest, she wanted to help," Karen smiled. "She loves story time at the library. And I didn't realise you can borrow DVDs there, too."

CHAPTER 5

Suddenly music filled the air. Summer turned to see a brass band marching into the square, with I-Lin at the front!

"When I told the band about your protest, they wanted to help," I-Lin explained. "We get our sheet music from the library. And I didn't know you could borrow ebooks too – fantastic!"

"We need the library!" everyone cried.

23

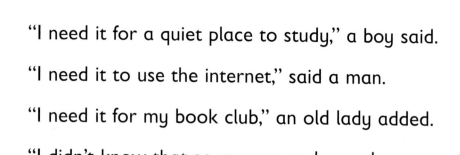

"I need it for a quiet place to study," a boy said.

"I need it to use the internet," said a man.

"I need it for my book club," an old lady added.

"I didn't know that so many people need the library," Summer gasped.

"Neither did I," said a voice. It was the Mayor.

"If all these people need the library, we cannot close it," the Mayor said. "But we need to save money somehow."

"I volunteer to help at the library!"

a man shouted.

"Me too!" a lady raised her hand.

"We'll make donations," said others in the crowd.

"I have lots of books I'd like to give the library," an old man said.

"So do we!" others cried, putting up their hands. Soon lots of people had their hands in the air.

"Wonderful. Then the library can stay open." the Mayor cried.

NO MORE
LIBRARY
CLOSING
DOWN

WE SAVED OUR LIBRARY

"Hurray!" everyone cheered.

"Well done, Summer," Karen said. "You saved
the library!"

"No," Summer smiled, looking around.

"We all did."

Things to think about

1. How does Summer find out about the library closing?
2. How does she feel about it?
3. Why does Summer's Mum suggest holding a protest?
4. How does Summer help people realise why having a local library is so important?
5. How do you think Summer feels after the protest?

Write it yourself

One of the themes in this story is protesting. Now try to write your own story about a similar theme.

Plan your story before you begin to write it.
Start off with a story map:
• a beginning to introduce the characters and where your story is set (the setting);
• a problem which the main characters will need to fix in the story;
• an ending where the problems are resolved.

Get writing! Try to use interesting phrases such as "Suddenly, music filled the air" to describe your story world and excite your reader.

Notes for parents and carers

Independent reading
This series is designed to provide an opportunity for your child to read independently, for pleasure and enjoyment. These notes are written for you to help your child make the most of this book.

About the book
Summer is upset when she finds out her local library is going to close down. She sets about organising a protest, with the help of her mum. If enough people know about the plan, surely they can save the library!

Before reading
Ask your child why they have selected this book. Look at the title and blurb together. What do they think it will be about? Do they think they will like it?

During reading
Encourage your child to read independently. If they get stuck on a word, remind them that they can sound it out in syllable chunks. They can also read on in the sentence and think about what would make sense.

After reading
Support comprehension and help your child think about the messages in the book that go beyond the story, using the questions on the page opposite.
Give your child a chance to respond to the story, asking:
Did you enjoy the story and why?
Who was your favourite character?
What was your favourite part?
What did you expect to happen at the end?

Franklin Watts
First published in Great Britain in 2018
by The Watts Publishing Group

Series Editors: Jackie Hamley and Melanie Palmer
Series Advisors: Dr Sue Bodman and Glen Franklin
Series Designer: Peter Scoulding

A CIP catalogue record for this book is
available from the British Library.

ISBN 978 1 4451 6308 6 (hbk)
ISBN 978 1 4451 6309 3 (pbk)
ISBN 978 1 4451 6307 9 (library ebook)

Printed in China

Franklin Watts
An imprint of
Hachette Children's Group
Part of The Watts Publishing Group
Carmelite House
50 Victoria Embankment
London EC4Y 0DZ

An Hachette UK Company
www.hachette.co.uk

www.franklinwatts.co.uk

FSC
www.fsc.org
MIX
Paper from
responsible sources
FSC® C104740